KV-394-897

1 85103 045 X

First published 1987 by Editions Gallimard
First published 1988 in Great Britain by Moonlight Publishing Ltd,
131 Kensington Church Street, London W8
© 1987 by Editions Gallimard
English text © 1988 by Moonlight Publishing Ltd

Printed in Italy by Editoriale Libraria

UNIFORMS
THROUGH THE AGES
A HISTORY OF COSTUME: VOL 2

DISCOVERERS

Written and illustrated by
Jean-Louis Besson

Translated by Sarah Matthews

MOONLIGHT PUBLISHING

Contents

The Flood, as described in the Bible

Prince Meskalamdu's golden helmet

Five thousand years ago, as the floods subsided, the first tendrils of Western civilisation began to grow. In the valleys of the Tigris and the Euphrates, the Sumerians – inventors of writing and of the wheel – built towns and, to defend the towns, set up the first armies. The foot soldiers formed up in ranks of six. They dressed in a fringed tunic which left the right arm bare. Their officers wore a strip of studded leather over one shoulder. This provided protection for their chests and bellies. According to their rank, the soldiers had helmets of leather, of bronze, or of gold. The war-chariots moved very slowly, drawn by onagers, huge half-wild asses.

1800 B.C. Invaders from the north, Hurrites, or from Asia, Hittites, spread knowledge of a skill they themselves had learned from other nomadic peoples in far off Mongolia: the use of horses as mounts rather than as meals.

A light two-wheeled chariot became a swift, manoeuvrable war machine. **The Assyrians** used it and cavalry side by side, with impressive efficiency: two soldiers rode the same horse, one to guide the animal, the other to wield the weapons. The archers in their chariots wore a long tunic fastened with a belt at the waist.

For horse-riding, trousers proved convenient, worn with shin-guards and high boots. On top, a short breastplate of metal scales, finished off with a pointed helmet lined with leather.

Ziggurat, a temple that also served as an astronomical observatory

The King of Akkad, Naramsu'en, wore a horned helmet, a privilege reserved for gods and princes.

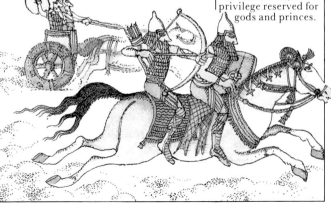

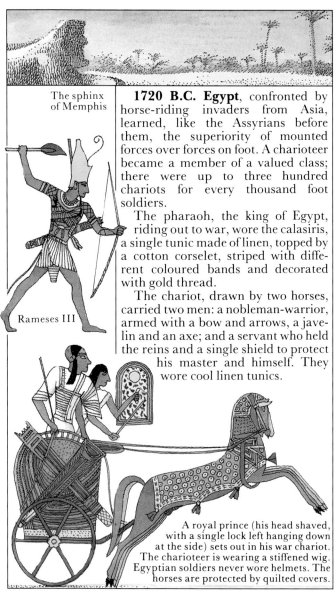

The sphinx of Memphis

Rameses III

1720 B.C. Egypt, confronted by horse-riding invaders from Asia, learned, like the Assyrians before them, the superiority of mounted forces over forces on foot. A charioteer became a member of a valued class; there were up to three hundred chariots for every thousand foot soldiers.

The pharaoh, the king of Egypt, riding out to war, wore the calasiris, a single tunic made of linen, topped by a cotton corselet, striped with different coloured bands and decorated with gold thread.

The chariot, drawn by two horses, carried two men: a nobleman-warrior, armed with a bow and arrows, a javelin and an axe; and a servant who held the reins and a single shield to protect his master and himself. They wore cool linen tunics.

A royal prince (his head shaved, with a single lock left hanging down at the side) sets out in his war chariot. The charioteer is wearing a stiffened wig. Egyptian soldiers never wore helmets. The horses are protected by quilted covers.

520 B.C. The Persian army became the best in the world, largely thanks to its host of mounted archers which included the ten thousand 'Immortals' of the royal guard. Shouldering their bows, they wore tight trousers and long tunics embroidered with patterns and flowers, held in at the waist with coloured sashes which showed off the long hanging sleeves of the tunic.

Less grand archers wore a shorter, simpler tunic over their trousers. These tunics were not so highly decorated and were cut to fit.

Babylon, on the banks of the Euphrates

Persian archer: he is wearing a cap of felt

Archers of the royal guard

Soldiers hiding inside the Trojan horse

The Amazons were said to cut off one breast, to handle their weapons more easily

For **the Greeks**, it was everybody's job to defend the city. The infantry – hoplites – were all equal soldier-citizens. In combat, they formed up in a square with sixty-four men along each side: the phalanxes.

Their whole armour, or panoply, was made up of a leather breastplate, reinforced with bronze plates, worn over a short tunic. Greaves, made of leather or metal, protected their shins and knees. On their feet they wore studded sandals and on their heads a helmet with cheek-guards and an impressive crest.

Hoplites

490 B.C. The Battle of Marathon, to the north-east of Athens. Ten thousand hoplites repulsed the invasion of a vastly superior Persian force. The victory was due in great part to the phalanxes, whose shields, held not only by a hand-grip but with a loop over the forearm, could be turned to provide continuous protection for the length of the rank.

For several hundred years the Greek phalanx served as a model for the infantry of Europe, and of other parts of the world.

A runner ran 42 750 km, to tell Athens of the victory: the first marathon.

Boetian helmet

Kyne, a light leather helmet with a wooden point.

The shield was decorated with a sign of the zodiac and hung with a sheet of painted cloth.

The Corinthian helmet could be worn in two positions: off the face, as here, or lowered to cover the face in combat.

Hoplite trumpeter

13

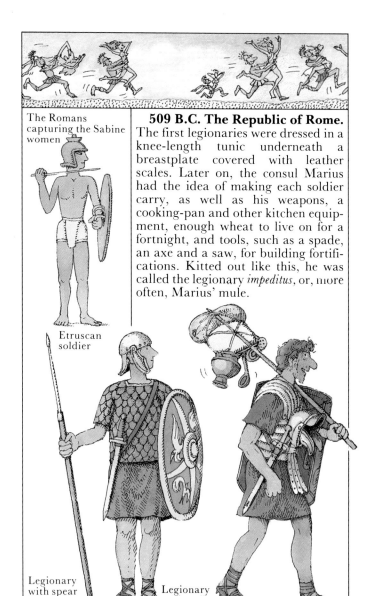

The Romans capturing the Sabine women

509 B.C. The Republic of Rome.
The first legionaries were dressed in a knee-length tunic underneath a breastplate covered with leather scales. Later on, the consul Marius had the idea of making each soldier carry, as well as his weapons, a cooking-pan and other kitchen equipment, enough wheat to live on for a fortnight, and tools, such as a spade, an axe and a saw, for building fortifications. Kitted out like this, he was called the legionary *impeditus*, or, more often, Marius' mule.

Etruscan soldier

Legionary with spear and sword

Legionary *impeditus*

390 B.C. The Gauls reached Italy. Gradually the Romans adopted the fashion of wearing short trousers like their northern neighbours. From now on their breastplates were made of bands of metal around the chest, with others coming down and covering the shoulders. The officers wore helmets decorated with feathers. Centurions carried in their hands, as a badge of office, a vine branch which could be used as an effective enforcer of discipline. This is the origin of the field-marshal's baton of today.

The Gauls were about to attack! The sacred geese on the Roman Capitol gave the alarm.

Trajan's breastplate: two bronze plates joined with metal links

Centurion   Tribune

The legionaries made a 'tortuga', or shelter, by locking their shields above their heads to protect them

250 B.C. The Roman Army: once the citizens no longer provided their own arms at their own cost and according to their own ideas, the Roman legion became the first coherently organised army. Made up of 6000 men, commanded by a general, it was divided into ten cohorts each led by a tribune. Every cohort was divided in turn into three manipules of 200 men, each made up of two centuries of 100 men, with each century commanded by a centurion.

Each legion had its cavalry, its front rank spearsmen, its second rank, and its rear-guard of veterans. It also had its own band: drums, trumpets, tubas, horns, flutes, tambourines and bells.

As well as banners, every legion carried its own precious sacred symbol: the silver eagle.

For the next five hundred years, there was no better fighting unit.

218 B.C. Hannibal crossed the Alps with 50 000 infantry, 9 000 cavalry and 37 elephants.

Feast days, victory celebrations, national funerals, were all good excuses to go to the circus and watch the gladiators. Gladiators were often prisoners of war, or men who had been condemned to death.

They had different specialities, and different costumes: the *bestiarius*, who fought wild animals, wore nothing but a loin-cloth, while the *mirmillon* had a sword and shield and an elaborate helmet completely covering his face.

The *retiarius* fought with a net and a trident. He had a special high collar of bronze attached to his shoulders to protect his head and neck.

The *mirmillon* had his right arm covered with articulated metal bands.

Unlike the Romans, **the Angles** wore whatever they liked. Some preferred to fight bare-chested, while others wore animal-skin tunics. They all wore their hair in plaits, so that it would not get in their way when they were fighting, and they all had trousers of varying lengths, which narrowed at mid-calf. The leather helmets of their forefathers had given way to metal helmets decorated with crests and wings and horns. Further north, the Caledonians flung themselves into battle wearing little more than their elaborate tattoos.

Hadrian's Wall, about **AD 120**

Caledonian

Angle warriors

Attila and his hordes swept into Europe from Mongolia, restless, land-hungry and brilliant horsemen. A contemporary historian described the battle which halted their onslaught as the most 'ferocious, confused, monstrous and unremitting combat the world had ever seen'.

AD 395 The Huns invaded the Roman empire. Their carefully cultivated ferocity and their exceptional riding ability on the swift, enduring little Asian ponies made them redoubtable opponents. They wore trousers, far more practical for riding than skirts.

Over their trousers they wore tunics which had been cut and sewn together, most often from leather or animal skins.

Attila and his hordes

Europe was occupied by the Alamans, the Franks, the Saxons and the Vandals, different tribes who had followed Attila into the rich lands of what once was the Roman empire. Only the leaders wore helmets. The ordinary soldiers wore nothing on their heads but their heavy plaits – some of them even shaved the backs of their heads, leaving a topknot at the front. Their shoes were fastened with cross-gartering which also kept up the bands of cloth which they wrapped round their legs instead of trousers.

Outposts of the Roman empire in Britain and Gaul fell easy prey to the fighters from Asia.

A sleeveless tunic of animal skin served as a breast-plate.

Frankish warriors

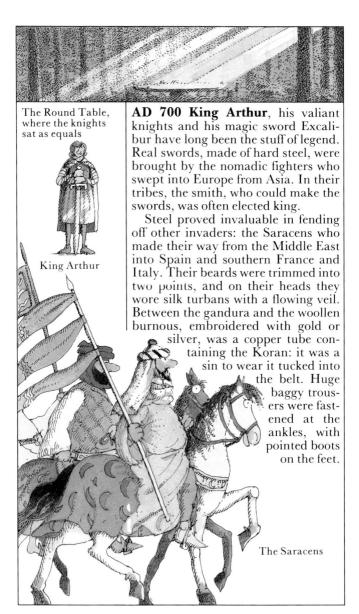

The Round Table, where the knights sat as equals

King Arthur

AD 700 King Arthur, his valiant knights and his magic sword Excalibur have long been the stuff of legend. Real swords, made of hard steel, were brought by the nomadic fighters who swept into Europe from Asia. In their tribes, the smith, who could make the swords, was often elected king.

Steel proved invaluable in fending off other invaders: the Saracens who made their way from the Middle East into Spain and southern France and Italy. Their beards were trimmed into two points, and on their heads they wore silk turbans with a flowing veil. Between the gandura and the woollen burnous, embroidered with gold or silver, was a copper tube containing the Koran: it was a sin to wear it tucked into the belt. Huge baggy trousers were fastened at the ankles, with pointed boots on the feet.

The Saracens

AD 732 The Battle of Poitiers. The French, under Charles Martel, held back the Moorish invasion with a wall of steel: cavalrymen wearing a hood and cape of mail over a leather skirt. Others preferred to wear a tunic, sewn with a metal 'webbing'. Their helmets were of boiled leather or, more often, of metal with a nose-piece coming down to protect the face.

Unlike the former light cavalry of archers, the new heavy cavalry was equipped for hand-to-hand combat. Its armour was expensive and it soon became an exclusive group. Mounted fighters, or **knights**, became a small, wealthy and very soon a dominant class.

Dawn rises over the opposing camps on the plain of Poitiers.

Charles Martel's troops

1066 The Normans conquer England. The story of their achievement was commemorated in a long embroidered tapestry still to be seen in the Museum at Bayeux in France.

Metal discs rivetted to leather were replaced by rings sewn onto tough cloth. This was the byrnie worn by the Normans. It was a one-piece garment with hood, long sleeves and a long skirt, split for mounting on horseback. The hauberk was made of proper chain-mail, with thin metal rods forged into links as if they had been knitted together. The hauberk was very strong and flexible and immensely heavy. The shields were painted with identifying marks associated with each family: the beginnings of heraldry.

Norman soldiers

The byrnie: metal rings sewn onto a cloth tunic

The hauberk: the chain-mail was forged into inter-locking links.

24

1099 The beginning of the Crusades. Crusaders wore a cross – white for the English, red for the French, green for the Flemish – sewn onto their hauberks or their surcoats. Surcoats were cloth tunics worn over the hauberks, to help prevent the metal heating up, or glinting in the sun, which might reveal their position to the enemy. Helmets, or helms, were boxes laced up behind, with little holes drilled in them so that the wearer could see, hear, and more or less breathe. They were too heavy to be worn in real fighting and were reserved for tournaments.

On their way, the Crusaders met the Assassins.

The Assassins' mission was to kill all unbelievers.

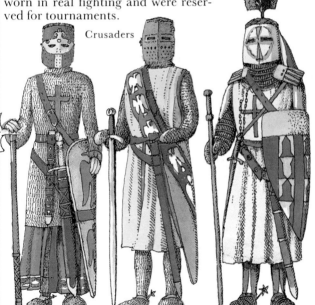

Crusaders

1346 Canons were first used in Europe at the battle of Crécy.

Some knights favoured a helmet with a long pointed snout: a basinet. This gave more room to breathe, and deflected blows away from the face and neck.

The Hundred Years' War. Infantry started to wear a light, wide-brimmed helmet over their chain-mail hoods. More and more popular was plate armour, made of shaped metal laced and rivetted together, to protect arms and legs. In Paris, the militia was dressed in the newly established city colours: red and blue. A pointed helmet covered the head and eyes and the leather corselet was rivetted with metal plates. Over it all, a flamboyantly scalloped cloak.

Foot soldier

Captain of the new Paris militia

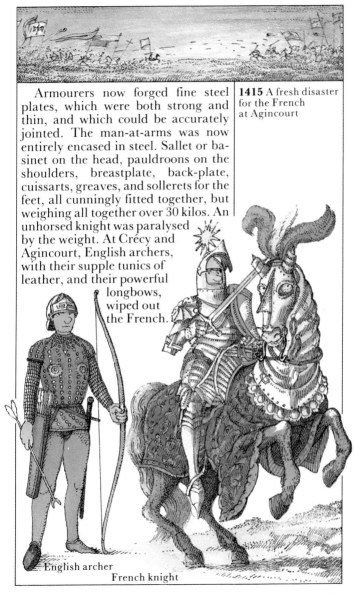

Armourers now forged fine steel plates, which were both strong and thin, and which could be accurately jointed. The man-at-arms was now entirely encased in steel. Sallet or basinet on the head, pauldroons on the shoulders, breastplate, back-plate, cuissarts, greaves, and sollerets for the feet, all cunningly fitted together, but weighing all together over 30 kilos. An unhorsed knight was paralysed by the weight. At Crécy and Agincourt, English archers, with their supple tunics of leather, and their powerful longbows, wiped out the French.

1415 A fresh disaster for the French at Agincourt

English archer
French knight

27

Plate armour was too heavy for fighting in, but was perfect for **tournaments**, where two knights on horseback thundered towards one another and sought to unhorse the other with blunted lances. Under the interested eyes of the ladies, it was not only the knights' skill and courage which were in question – the colours of their panoplies, the shine of the armour, the imaginativeness of their devices were all in competition too.

On their heads, they boasted helms or basinets

decorated with plumes and crests and brightly coloured
ribbons which floated out behind. On their left arms they
carried light shields painted with the coats of arms which
had become established since the Crusaders. The exotic
jousting costumes inspired the gaudy colours and parti-
coloured hose of the man-about-court.

The horses were decorated too, with a metal headband
carrying plumes or an emblem, a bridle hung with
brightly embroidered cloth, a saddle with a high padded
pommel and crupper, and a flowing saddle-cloth made up
in the knight's colours.

15th and 16th centuries

Henry VIII and his horse in full armour. The armour Henry VIII wore as a young man can still be seen in the Armoury of the Tower of London.

Even his moustache wore armour! The elaborate armour of the Emperor Maximilian

Swiss captain

German foot-soldier

Swiss guards

Swiss and German mercenaries who hired out their professional skills to the princes of Europe preferred to wear well-padded tunics and breeches rather than armour.

1492 Christopher Columbus lands in the New World.

A reiter, a German mercenary horse-soldier, with his special weapons, the lance and the pistol.

Halberdier

Arquebusier

Scots guard

Turkish janissary

The last vestige of metal armour was the breastplate or cuirass. Tears in the sleeves of a man's tunic, slashed by sword or pike, bore witness to the dangers he had faced. They gave rise to fashionable 'slashings' in court clothes.

German military musicians

First he put on a loin cloth, followed by a long loose shirt and silk trousers. Next he wore a hat and fighting-glove.

On his right side, he wore an arm-guard. His left sleeve was folded back and covered with an additional sleeve of mail.

The rest of his leather armour was fitted on and tied with thongs.

Next came a second pair of trousers, leggings and shoes.

A dagger, a curved sword, a long wooden bow and a lacquered quiver. The archer was armed.

1549 Portuguese sailors landed in Japan. The West was discovering the Far East. Here we see a **Japanese archer** getting ready for combat.

A gunner taking aim

German drummer

1600 Improvements in **firearms** made increasing demands on military mobility, and finally made armour redundant. From that time, infantry was divided into pikemen and arquebusiers. Puffy sleeves and breeches were still in fashion. As well as a sword worn on the left hip, a dagger tucked into the belt at the back provided a means of defence in close combat. On peaceful occasions, gentlemen meeting clasped each other by the right hand to prove they were unarmed.

Captain of the French King's Guard of Honour

Swiss guard

Waistcoats of buffalo or deer skin replaced the corselet. High-topped boots first came in. Musketeers, with their heavy muskets, wore bandoliers strung with charges of powder and shot. Officers adopted the habit of wearing scarves in their national colours: blue for Sweden, orange for the Netherlands, white for France, red for Cromwell's New Model Army. Privates simply wore a ribbon or a cockade.

Gustavus Adolphus of Sweden, the first monarch to dress his soldiers in uniform

Officer

French Musketeer

Feathers, cockades and swirling cloak: a true swashbuckler.

1660 The Restoration. Charles II disbanded Cromwell's army of professional soldiers and created new regiments of loyal Royalist troops: the Coldstream Guards in 1660, and the mounted Life Guards and the Horse Guards Blue in 1661. The Blues were so-called after the dark blue of the coat-of-arms of the man who raised them, the Earl of Oxford. On the Continent, the young French king, Louis XIV, paraded before his troops in a contemporary version of the dress of a Roman emperor.

Swiss guard

Louis XIV, the French 'Sun King', as a Roman emperor

The era of national military uniforms began in Europe. At first, uniforms did not look much different from civilian clothes, apart from the colours used. Soldiers wore long coats, breeches, gaiters, cravats and three-cornered hats – all the material for their clothes could be bought in bulk, which made them much cheaper. At the same time, the fact that his clothes, his equipment and his weapons had all been provided for him by his monarch reminded a soldier where his loyalties lay.

1685 The Monmouth rebellion

Generals had no taste for wearing uniforms. They tended to prefer gold embroidery on their sleeves to mark their wealth and status.

Musketeer

Infantry officer

General

New fortifications built in zigzags raked an approaching enemy with deadly gunfire.

1690 The invention of a new weapon, the grenade, thrown by a specialised soldier, the grenadier.

The English noticed that a brimless hat ran less risk of catching the soldier's arm as he was throwing his grenade. To leave both arms free, the grenadier carried his ammunition and his flintlock slung on straps across his chest.

Someone had the idea of fixing his dagger, or Bayonne knife, to the end of his flintlock in order to have a weapon to hand when his ammunition ran out or he was too hard-pressed to reload: the bayonet was invented.

French grenadier   English grenadier

A short time before, the cavalry had taken on a new addition, the dragoon. Dragoons differed from the rest in that they did not have any one particular skill: they were created to fight as well on foot as on horseback. They wore high bonnets and heavy boots.

Hussars first came from Hungary. Superb horsemen, they wore short jackets, high boots and fur hats. They quickly earned a reputation for great skill and high tempers.

Barefoot colonial guard

Dragoon

Hussar

Frederick the Great, in uniform, reviews the Prussian Guard.

1730 Frederick the Great of Prussia, called the Sergeant-King, recruited his soldiers throughout Europe and established a regiment of grenadiers all over six feet tall. Their high hats decorated with copper insignia emphasised their impressive appearance.

Prussian grenadiers wore blue, the British red, the French white. The colours of the reveres distinguished the separate regiments.

A towering grenadier

French colour-sergeant and fusilier

Military musicians arrayed them-selves in dashing costumes covered in gold and silver braid and ribbons. Those who kept up their comrades' courage during a charge by playing the flute or beating the drum were all the braver for having no weapons of their own, and for having to maintain the morale of others when their own might be gone. They were often, too, the target of attacks by the enemy, who coveted their instruments.

1745 The Battle of Fontenoy. Lord Charles Hay called to his opponents to fire first: 'Messieurs les gardes françaises, tirez', to which came the reply: 'We never fire first. Fire first yourselves!'

Equerry

Cymbals

Kettle drums

1776 The thirteen British colonies which had been set up in North America proclaimed their independence and found themselves at war with King George III.

The British army wore their customary red coats and white breeches, apart from the Scots regiments, who kept the kilt. Their German allies were usually dressed in blue, with blue and white striped trousers. The other British allies, the Iroquois, wore leather and tattoos.

The new American Congress chose its first leader, Washington, and a new flag, the stars and stripes, with thirteen stars and thirteen stripes to represent the thirteen states.

Congress troops were dressed in blue or brown. Minutemen and riflemen wore hunting clothes, with a sprig of laurel tucked into their hats to distinguish them from the loyalists.

After a time the French came and helped the Americans in the final victory of Yorktown.

1794 The young French Republic found itself surrounded by hostile monarchist states anxious to show their own inhabitants that revolution and the killing of kings was not an example to be followed. The French hastened· to defend their new red, white and blue flag. The throng could not all be catered for in the available uniforms, and so they tended to dress themselves as best they could. All, however, wore a cockade or a sash in the national colours.

Republican
balloonist

Artilleryman

Grenadier
of the
French
National
Guard

Volunteer of the
Parisian National
Guard

General. His sash
went round his waist
several times and was
fastened on the hip in
a knot.

44

Not all the enemies of the Republic were outside the borders of France. In the Vendée, monarchist resistance persisted. The monarchists usually wore civilian clothes, the better to slip away and merge into the general population. In combat, however, they sported their own identifying badges. Locally woven scarves were wound round the head, and, for the leaders, round the waist as well, and, above all, the symbol of the Sacred Heart was pinned to the chest.

1796 Bonaparte's victory at Arcole

The Paris flag: Liberty or Death.

Austrian fusilier and grenadier

A Vendée resistance leader

The French army in Egypt, led by Bonaparte, raised a dromedary regiment.

1805 The sun rises over the battlefield of Austerlitz.

What is war? A barbarian's job calling for nothing more than being the strongest at a given time in a given place.

Napoleon

Leaders must always be distinguishable from their subordinates. Napoleon I let his officers adorn themselves with gold braid and feathers in their hats; he wore the simple uniform of a light infantryman, made of green cloth with red facings!

The grenadiers of the Imperial Guard were at least 5 foot 10 inches tall, without their bearskin hats. Smaller soldiers were recruited into a bantam rifle regiment. The mamelukes accompanied Napoleon on his return from his Egyptian campaign. They stayed with him and formed a most spectacular escort.

Mameluke

Grenadier and bantam rifleman

The Russian army

Cossack

Grenadiers

Dragoon
and hussar

Infantry
man

General

Tsar
Alexander I

Emperor
Napoleon I

The French army

Marshal of France   Brigadier   Infantryman   Artilleryman

1809 Capture of Saragossa

Dragoon in stable fatigues

The cavalry of Napoleon's Grande Armée gleamed and glowed with every colour of the rainbow. Jackets with gold frogging, pelisses flung from one shoulder, elaborately embroidered breeches, decorated sashes, sumptuous saddlecloths, busbies, shakos, lancer caps, crested helmets . . .

Dragoon cornet

Polish lancer

Cavalryman

Hussar

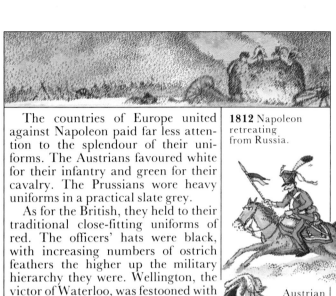

The countries of Europe united against Napoleon paid far less attention to the splendour of their uniforms. The Austrians favoured white for their infantry and green for their cavalry. The Prussians wore heavy uniforms in a practical slate grey.

As for the British, they held to their traditional close-fitting uniforms of red. The officers' hats were black, with increasing numbers of ostrich feathers the higher up the military hierarchy they were. Wellington, the victor of Waterloo, was festooned with feathers.

1812 Napoleon retreating from Russia.

Austrian uhlan

Prussian infantryman

Wellington

Austrian fusilier

English foot-soldier of the line

Lieutenant-general

The army of
occupation in Paris

Both France and
England had special
Hospitals for army
veterans.

1815 The three years' occupation of Paris gave the erstwhile opponents a chance to admire each others' uniforms rather than trying to pierce them with steel or shot. The monarchy was restored to the throne of France. The new king, Louis XVIII, was faced with the problem of obliterating memories of Napoleonic glory while avoiding the creation of masses of unhappy unemployed soldiers. He also needed to restore a sense of French national pride. The army was given a new look – blue and white became the dominant colours, the Royalist fleur-de-lys and Louis' initial replaced the Napoleonic eagle and the letter N.

Cartridge-pouch of the French National Guard

Uniforms in the British Army also changed after Waterloo: the infantry and foot artillery took to the bell-topped French shako, although fur caps continued to be worn by fusiliers and grenadiers. By 1822, trousers instead of breeches were usual.

Armies abroad gradually adapted to foreign conditions – one of the most radical departures was the cap designed by the French Marshal Bugeaud to keep the sun off the heads of his troops in Algeria. The shape he worked out formed the basis of the kepi worn by French gendarmes to this day.

The prototype kepi designed by Marshal Bugeaud

French infantryman in the new madder-red trousers

Officer in the Royal Guard

1854 The Crimean War. The British army which set sail for the East in the spring of 1854 did so in their uncomfortable and impractical full dress. Gradually, the longer they were in Turkey, the more concessions they made to the climate. First cloths covered their helmets, then epaulettes, shakos and stocks were abandoned. In the end, new uniforms, designed by Prince Albert, were sent out.

Everyone discovered the practicality of wearing stripes on the sleeve to indicate rank.

British sailor

Zouave

Rifleman of the French Foreign Legion

Infantry officer

1857 The Indian Mutiny. Moslem sepoys, or native soldiers, in the Indian army, mutinied. It took time and intense fighting before the British will prevailed. It was found that the traditional British redcoats made too easy a target for sharpshooters, and a change was proposed to a dustcoloured uniform – 'khaki' in Hindustani.

In Algeria, the French too employed native troops – spahis (from the same Persian word as 'sepoy'). The most exotic-looking were the baggy-trousered zouaves.

French sapper

Canteen-girl, clad in practical trousers and feminine skirt

British infantryman in full dress and battle-dress

Lancer of the Imperial Guard

The flag of the Union. Thirteen stripes represent the original thirteen states, while each star represents a state of the Union.

1861 The American Civil War.

Thirteen southern states, quarrelling with the North's determination to declare slavery illegal, decided to leave the Union and set up their own Confederacy.

All the northern troops, whether infantry, cavalry, artillery or navy, wore the same dark blue uniform, with lighter blue trousers and a wide-brimmed hat. The hat soon proved impractical for the infantry and was replaced by a soft forage cap. Only the cavalry kept the wide-brimmed black felt hat, with its regulation chin-strap fastened at the front.

The Confederate army chose grey for their jackets and sky-blue for their trousers. They too favoured the comfort and practicality of the forage cap.

As the war progressed, their uniforms became more and more individualised. Having no industry, they could not manufacture cloth and, as imports from Europe were blockaded, clothes became very much a matter of make-do and mend by wives and sweethearts at home.

1862 Naval battle between the frigate *Virginia* and the Union ironclad *Monitor*

The Confederates from the southern states

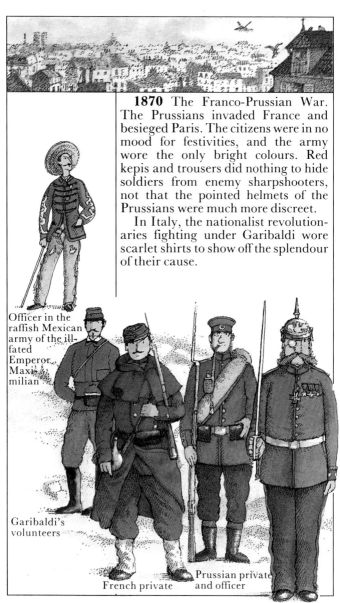

1870 The Franco-Prussian War. The Prussians invaded France and besieged Paris. The citizens were in no mood for festivities, and the army wore the only bright colours. Red kepis and trousers did nothing to hide soldiers from enemy sharpshooters, not that the pointed helmets of the Prussians were much more discreet.

In Italy, the nationalist revolutionaries fighting under Garibaldi wore scarlet shirts to show off the splendour of their cause.

Officer in the raffish Mexican army of the ill-fated Emperor Maximilian

Garibaldi's volunteers

French private

Prussian private and officer

The British army was caught between two worlds: in the Sudan, cavalry charges recalled a distant age of chivalry; the Boer War taught a valuable lesson in the crucial importance of the rifle and the Maxim gun. When not on parade, the army adopted khaki wholesale. Some, like the Bengal lancers, wore the drab colour with a certain dash.

On the Continent, there was a reaction towards finery, with braid and buttons proliferating even on an officer's undress uniform.

1884 Gunship at Tonkin

In every army, marching songs gave the troops a chance to voice their feelings.

Marine
Bengal lancer

Cavalry officer

1914 The beginning of the First World War, the Great War, the War to End Wars. Invaded by the Germans, the French set off for the Battle of the Marne by taxi, still decked out in the colourful uniforms of the nineteenth century. Trench warfare and enemy snipers soon emphasised the desirability of camouflage – though some, like the French colonial troops and the Italian bersaglieri with their splendid hats, disdained it. Rapidly rediscovered, too, was the usefulness of helmets – although not for British officers. Their flat caps and Sam Browne belts marked them out as targets.

Spahi

Senegalese rifleman

British officer

Italian bersagliere

Russian infantryman

On both sides, uniforms and equipment became increasingly functional, as, for instance, the lamp attached to the Austrian infantryman's rifle, ready to illuminate his way on night marches.

The Germans were keen on retaining their spiked helmets – even the dismounted uhlans still wore their highly polished shapskas, though covered with a cloth to make them less visible in battle.

All these impractical ornaments were the last remnants of a doomed era.

'Big Bertha', an enormous canon brought up on rails by the Germans to bombard Paris

Uhlan

German officer

Austrian infantryman

Bulgarian officer

Turk

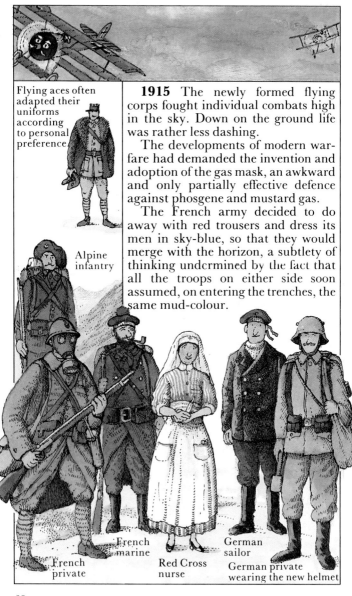

Flying aces often adapted their uniforms according to personal preference.

Alpine infantry

1915 The newly formed flying corps fought individual combats high in the sky. Down on the ground life was rather less dashing.

The developments of modern warfare had demanded the invention and adoption of the gas mask, an awkward and only partially effective defence against phosgene and mustard gas.

The French army decided to do away with red trousers and dress its men in sky-blue, so that they would merge with the horizon, a subtlety of thinking undermined by the fact that all the troops on either side soon assumed, on entering the trenches, the same mud-colour.

French private

French marine

Red Cross nurse

German sailor

German private wearing the new helmet

1917 The invention of the first tanks called for new equipment. Allied troops in battle gave rise to curious adaptations of traditional dress – khaki aprons over the kilt and sand-coloured turbans amongst them.

The arrival of the Americans brought a new wide-brimmed hat onto the scene. It was under his traditional kepi, though, that Foch rode through Paris in the victory parade in 1918.

English tank crewman wearing anti-explosion mask

Indian cavalryman

Japanese

Scots private in battle-dress

American 'doughboy'

Marshal Foch

1933 Nuremberg rally

The Fascist party in Italy, and the National Socialists, or Nazis, in Germany, seized power, borne along on a tide of popular fervour and helped by bands of militaristic, uniform-wearing supporters. Blackshirts, storm-troopers, Hitler youth, all wore trimly cut uniforms, arrayed with belts and buckles and brassards, all designed to inspire fear and respect for the leader, who was saluted with a click of the heels and a straight-arm salute.

In France and England, the armies did not seek to inspire fear.

Vittore-Emmanuel III, King of Italy, in traditional full dress uniform

Blackshirt

Storm trooper

Hitler youth

German airforce marshal

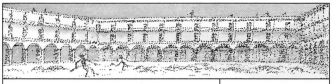

The lessons of the First World War were well learned. The emphasis was on camouflage and high-technology equipment – except on the parade-ground. There, finery still held sway, with officer cadets from Sandhurst and Saint-Cyr looking magnificent in their trim blue and red, the spahis glowing in their scarlet cloaks, and the Guards' regiments towering impressively over the tourists as they stood on duty outside Buckingham Palace.

1936 Spanish Civil War

The Gardia Civil wore flat black hats, the army pointed caps.

French Foreign Legion

Spahi

Cadet from Saint-Cyr

French general

Scots Guard

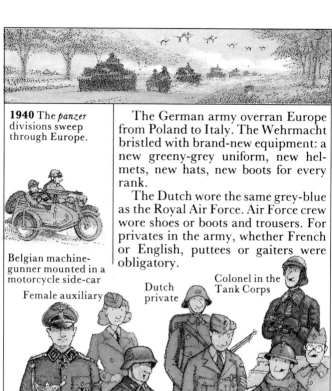

1940 The *panzer* divisions sweep through Europe.

The German army overran Europe from Poland to Italy. The Wehrmacht bristled with brand-new equipment: a new greeny-grey uniform, new helmets, new hats, new boots for every rank.

The Dutch wore the same grey-blue as the Royal Air Force. Air Force crew wore shoes or boots and trousers. For privates in the army, whether French or English, puttees or gaiters were obligatory.

Belgian machine-gunner mounted in a motorcycle side-car

Female auxiliary

Dutch private

Colonel in the Tank Corps

S.S. officer

Wehrmacht adjutant

R.A.F. pilot

French soldier with rubber galoshes

The war soon spread world-wide. American sailors in Hawaii wore their tropical kit, whites with a blue scarf. The marines, with their blue dress uniform, soon discarded elegance in favour of khaki battle-dress with a camouflage net across their helmets. It was not long before American bomber pilots set a trend for fur-lined jackets to keep the circulation going on their long unheated flights. His short jacket, and baggy trousers bound up to the knee with tight puttees, gave the Japanese soldier a distinctive silhouette.

1941 Pearl Harbour. The Japanese seek to destroy the US fleet.

Aircraft landing

Pilot

Marine in full dress

Marine in battle-dress

Japanese admiral and private soldier

American sailor

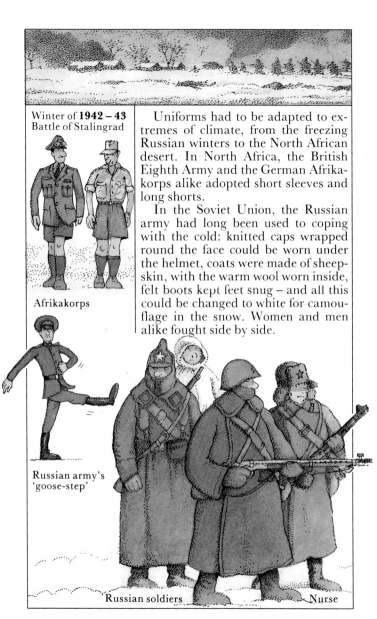

Winter of **1942 – 43**
Battle of Stalingrad

Afrikakorps

Russian army's
'goose-step'

Russian soldiers   Nurse

Uniforms had to be adapted to extremes of climate, from the freezing Russian winters to the North African desert. In North Africa, the British Eighth Army and the German Afrikakorps alike adopted short sleeves and long shorts.

In the Soviet Union, the Russian army had long been used to coping with the cold: knitted caps wrapped round the face could be worn under the helmet, coats were made of sheepskin, with the warm wool worn inside, felt boots kept feet snug – and all this could be changed to white for camouflage in the snow. Women and men alike fought side by side.

Military police

Parachutist in
battle-dress

U.S. generals

Free French
resistance
fighter

1945 Berlin was in ruins, the war was finally over. Generals and foot-soldiers alike wore battle-dress, with its practical provision of pockets: practicality was more important than show. It was as much working-clothes as uniform. Invented by the British, all armies soon adopted it.

As the victory parade marched through a liberated Paris, the French Foreign Legion brought up the rear, following its mascot, to be swept off, like other soldiers, to different wars and different ways . . .

French
collaborationist
soldier
from Vichy

With your guns and drums,
And drums and guns,
Johnny I hardly knew you . .
Traditional Irish song

67

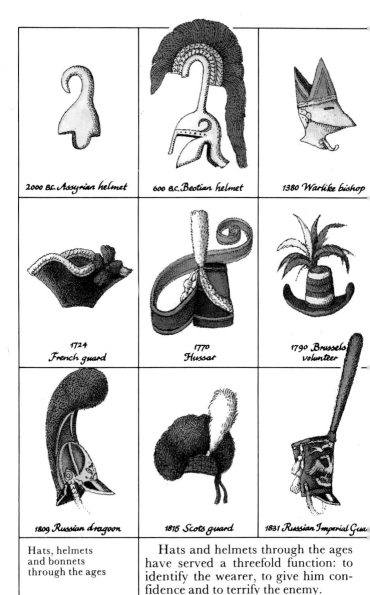

2000 B.C. *Assyrian helmet*

600 B.C. *Beotian helmet*

1380 *Warlike bishop*

1724 *French guard*

1770 *Hussar*

1790 *Brussels volunteer*

1809 *Russian dragoon*

1815 *Scots guard*

1831 *Russian Imperial Gua*

Hats, helmets and bonnets through the ages

Hats and helmets through the ages have served a threefold function: to identify the wearer, to give him confidence and to terrify the enemy.

1500 Dog-faced bassinet

1540 Jousting helmet

1550 Samurai helmet

1808
Spanish regiment

1808 Bashkir
in the Russian army

1809
Austrian grenadier

1845
Prussian Pickelhaube

1887 Dress helmet of an
officer of the Prussian Guard

1890
Italian Carabinere

Crested, plumed, cockaded, pointed, braided and brockaded, hats and helmets show vividly how soldiers saw themselves and wished to be seen.

Over four thousand years of warlike headgear . . .

An A to Z of Military Uniforms

Andrews' hat

An early attempt to solve the hat problem of the American army. The previous 'Hardee' hat had proved too hot and heavy, the kepi too insubstantial. The Andrews' hat was made of stone-coloured felt, with a wide brim. The design was soon modified to black velvet-finished fur, but, according to the unfortunate wearers, nothing redeemed it from quickly becoming under service conditions 'the most useless uncouth rag ever put upon a man's head'.

Basinet

Started life as a simple metal cap to protect the skull, but soon developed an additional mobile face-piece which could be lifted to survey the enemy and closed when he approached.

Baldric

Leather or cloth sash worn across the chest to support a sword or sabre.

Bicorne

Eighteenth-century round-crowned hat with brims turned up on both sides, which could be worn sideways on or with the points front and back, a style considered in the British army to be both more dashing and easier to keep on when riding.

Braiding

First adopted by officers in the eighteenth century, more as decoration than as a badge of rank, it has survived in all its golden splendour to become the 'scrambled egg' of today's top echelons.

Busby

Fur cap originally adapted from the Hungarians and introduced into the British army in the middle of the eighteenth century.

Calotte

Experimental helmet issued to the French at the start of the First World War. It was meant to fit inside the kepi, but it was so uncomfortable it was usually removed and used as a receptacle for water.

Cardigan

A long-sleeved woollen tunic buttoning up the front, named after Lord Cardigan, who first had such a garment made to keep him warm during the Crimean War.

Cartridge belt

First evolved by Indian-fighters in the American West. The development of rapid-firing repeating weapons meant that soldiers had to carry far more ammunition than before, while it was found almost impossible for troops to remove ammunition from a pouch without revealing their position. A waist-belt with loops for individual cartridges was developed. When it was found that the leather loops spoilt the metal cartridge-cases when they got wet, successful experiments were made with canvas. Webbing, the soldier's friend, had been born . . .

Crepeid
Laced boot worn by Greek infantry. The Roman version, *caligula*, gave the notorious Emperor his nickname when, as a child, his father's legion made him their mascot.

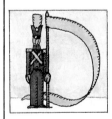

Death's Heads
Worn by the 17th Lancers at the Charge of the Light Brigade, and by the

Lützow 'Black Corps' as part of their 'gothick' apparel, together with black shakos, gloves and hanging plumes. During the First World War, the Kaiser's son, 'little Willy', was always depicted in British cartoons in the uniform of the 'Black Corps'.

Destrier
Warhorse ridden into battle by a medieval knight.

Dolmans
Short, much-braided jackets sported by hussars.

Doublets
Right into the seventeenth century, the Swiss Guard of the French King wore red, yellow and blue slashed doublets and brightly coloured codpieces.

Dragoons
Regiments created from infantry and mounted on horseback, they retained their infantry uniform with long coats and lapels.

Ear covers
Issued, together with cloth mittens, to the Prussian army in the nineteenth century.

Ensign
Officer carrying regimental flag.

Epaulettes
Strip of cloth buttoned across the shoulder. Some British officers in the Indian army substituted chain for cloth, in the belief that this would ward off sabre cuts.

Feathers
Originally worn as symbols of identification, they were found to be too easily copied when simply slipped into a hat-band, leading to unfortunate incidents of ambushes behind the lines. Persist as decoration to this day, particularly in ceremonial dress.

Feldgrau
The name of the 'field-grey' cloth and uniform in which the regular German army went to war in 1914.

Frogging
Gold braid worn across the chest, particularly favoured by cavalry regiments.

Fusil
A light musket or flintlock, which lent its name to those infantry regiments still called fusiliers.

Gaiters
In the eighteenth century, soldiers on campaign wore a second pair of stockings to keep the mud off their main pair. Gradually this second pair evolved into gaiters, which removed and laced or buckled up the back.

Gorget
Small crescent of metal worn originally as a protection for the neck.

Greatcoats
British army officers first adopted these from Russian eighteenth-century hussar officers, who wore long braided kaftans reaching almost to the ground.

Haversack
Originally the haysack in which the cavalry carried provisions for their horses, it soon came to be simply the stout canvas bag in which soldiers carried their own provisions.

Helm
Large wooden or metal helmet usually worn exclusively for tournaments, as it was much too cumbersome for combat.

Hoods
Issued to the British Foot Guards serving in America during the War of Independence, along with blanket-coats and leggings for winter wear.

Hussars
First appeared in Europe from Hungary after the defeat of the Turks at the gates of Vienna in 1683. The hussars were formed into regular regiments by the Austrians, under the leadership of hereditary chieftains A trickle of deserters

from the Austrian army found employment in the armies of Louis XIV of France. A corps of Royal Hussars was formed, but soon had to disband when its colonel lost it at cards.

Imperial Guard
Napoleon's Imperial Guard was the flower of his army, recruited from the most experienced soldiers. They were never defeated in combat until Waterloo, when they were held in reserve until the battle had already been lost.

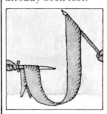

Jackets
Introduced for the cavalry about 1780, these started as short coats with high, wide cuffs and a border of lace down the front.

Jägers
German regiments

absorbed into the British army for colonial service overseas, particularly in the West Indies.

Jumpers
Loose tunics worn by the British infantry in India after the Indian mutiny. They came in red, blue, khaki or white. They were first made of cotton, but soon came to be knitted in wool.

Kaftans
First seen in Europe worn by Ukrainian Cossacks in Polish service, they were short, loose tunics worn over baggy trousers and soft boots. Even as early as the fourteenth century, the Cossacks wore their own distinctive uniform.

Kepi
Stiff round cap with a brim and a flat top, a lower, more practical version of the shako. During the nineteenth century it became a symbol of liberty as against the militaristic pickelhaube. It is still worn by the French army.

Lancers
Originally Saxon volunteers in the French army, uhlans with lances, their costume provided the inspiration for uniforms of lancer regiments everywhere. It was based on Polish national dress, and consisted of a fur-trimmed cap with a square crown, known as a shapska, and a long sleeveless coat. Their weapons were a lance with pennon, a curved sabre and pistol stuck into the belt at their waists.

Lapels
Developed from the buttoned-back facings of the 19th century double-breasted frock coat. Similar to the reveres which could be coloured to distinguish regiments.

Marines
In September 1803, Napoleon I raised a battalion of sailors to act as cover during his invasion of England. They remained in existence as the marines of the Guard, popularly known as the 'Naval Hussars'.

Moccasins
The British in America admired the practicality of this American Indian footwear and soon adapted them for the use of their own soldiers.

Moustache
Allowed in the British cavalry, but banned in the infantry.

N
Initial letter of Napoleon's name, used, with the Imperial eagle, as a distinguishing mark on every conceivable item of uniform and equipment in the armies of Napoleon I and Napoleon III.

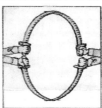

Overalls
Made in canvas, and issued to the British army during the American War of Independence.

Overcoats
During the Siege of Sebastopol, Russian officers, unable to obtain the capes they usually wore, adopted the soldiers' greatcoats. To mark their rank, they sewed strips of gold braid on to the shoulder-straps. This is the origin of shoulder-boards.

Palfrey
Parade horse used by medieval knights on ceremonial occasions.

Pantaloons
Worn by the British infantry at the start of the Napoleonic Wars with black calf-length gaiters.

Pelisse
Short, braided, fur-lined jacket worn by dragoons or hussars, slung unfastened over one shoulder.

Pickelhaube
Distinctive helmet with a sharp point on top, worn in the German army in the 19th and early 20th centuries.

Plastron
Steel breastplate worn beneath the hauberk.

Plumes
Made variously of feathers or horsehair, they were adopted in the seventeenth century as field-signs. They soon came to be used as regimental emblems, dyed in a range of striking and distinctive colours.

Pigtails
A very early reference to the use of pigtails occurs in 1684 when a colonel of the Scots Regiment of Foot Guards ordered his men to tie their hair back out of their eyes when firing.

Queen's Own Rangers
Copied by General Wolfe from such bodies as the Ranging Company of Colonel Blanchard's New Hampshire Provincial Regiment. Recruited from trappers and frontiersmen, they were expert woodsmen, often used in long-distance raids. They were the only troops to operate in winter, striding silently over snow-drifts in their snow-shoes.

Revolver cords
Worn by British cavalry during the Afghan Wars, along with pouch-belts, brown leather waist-belts, and brown Sam Brownes carrying their swords.

Roundheads
Members of Oliver Cromwell's New Model Army during the English Civil War. The suits of the men were ordered in bulk, and were usually made of strong material dyed in fast colours. At the battle of Edgehill there were

regiments dressed in red, blue, white, green, grey, purple and orange. Despite popular belief, the Roundheads had hair quite as long and clothes quite as fashionable as their Royalist opponents.

Sabretache
A sack carried from the sword belt which held useful equipment and plunder.

Sallet
Light medieval helmet with a slit in front to see through.

Sam Browne
A belt invented by General Sir Samuel J. Browne after he lost his arm in the Indian Mutiny. Finding great difficulty in carrying his sword when dismounted, he worked out a system of belt and crosspiece which would not only support his sword, but carry his pistol too.

Shako
Tall, flat-topped cap with a rigid peak, adapted from the Hungarian hussar's

hat, sometimes worn very tall and always worn with a plume.

Shorts
As early as 1908, the British army was wearing shorts, with stockings and puttees, in India and other hot weather stations.

Spatterdash
Early form of gaiter.

Sunhelmets
First introduced experimentally in the British Army during the Indian Mutiny. They were usually made of pith and were shaped in a crest which allowed air to circulate through the front. Curtains or a veil down the back protected the neck from possible sunstroke.

Tasset
Armour worn by pikemen in the seventeenth century to protect their thighs.

Tricolour
Red, white and blue emblem of the French Republic, in contrast to the monarchy's fleur-de-lys.

Triple-barred helmets
Seventeenth-century helmets copied from the Turks. An articulated metal 'tail' protected the back of the neck, while three bars coming down from the brim at the front protected the face but still allowed the wearer to see.

Turbans
The Egyptian campaign at the end of the eighteenth century had a great influence on dress. Sir William Sydney Smith is said to have arrived in London in flowing Arab robes and with the army despatches tucked into his turban.

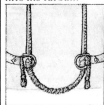

Uhlan
Originally Tartar horsemen, they gave their name to Austrian and German regiments of lancers, known for their courage and ferocity.

Ulanka
Tunic worn by Prussian Guard lancer regiment in the nineteenth century.

Umbo
Round, pointed centre to Roman shields.

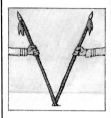

Vareuse
Loose shirt introduced experimentally into the French army at the turn of the century, along with a slouch hat and leather anklets. The experimental uniform was withdrawn by popular demand.

Visor
Hinged face-covering at the front of a helmet, which could be lifted and lowered.

Waffenrock
Short tunic, with a narrow, usually belted, waist, worn by the German army since the 19th century.

Waistcoats
First introduced in the 17th century, they began as 'vests' or undercoats of much the same cut and length as the coat itself, even sometimes with long sleeves which appeared below the coat cuffs. Soon they became shorter and tighter, with shallow pockets, or fobs, which could hold a watch.

Xerxes
Son of Darius, King of Persia, who was defeated at the battle of Marathon. When Xerxes succeeded his father in 485 B.C. he was determined to avenge his defeat.

Yeoman of the Guard
Veteran soldiers employed as Gentlemen Warders of the Tower of London. On ceremonial occasions they parade in the scarlet tunics and breeches which were the uniform when the Guard was first formed by Henry VIII in the 16th century. Because they are traditionally partly paid in a ration of beef, they are also called 'Beefeaters'.

Zouaves
French regiment originally formed from tribesmen of the Zouaoua tribe in Algeria.
The uniform of the zouaves became world-famous, with its red tasselled fez, wound round with a turban on ceremonial occasions, a blue waistcoat fastening at the back, a blue open-necked jacket and enormously baggy scarlet trousers tucked into yellow gaiters.

About the author-illustrator

Jean-Louis Besson was barely three years old in 1935, when the French army finally abandoned their sky-blue uniforms for the duller, more practical khaki.

Thirty years later, while working in an advertising agency helping to ensure the commercial success of jumpers, socks and knitting-wool, he was struck by the fascination of the colour and line of clothes. At this stage, he was particularly interested in civilian clothes – an interest which he has now expressed in **Clothes through the Ages**, the companion *Discoverers* volume in this **History of Costume**.

When that book was finished, he turned with delight and satisfaction to the history of military clothing.

A third book written and illustrated by Jean-Louis Besson and available in the *Discoverers* series is the witty and highly-informative **Discoveries and Inventions.**